ALL ABOUT DREAMS

WELCOME TO THE WORLD OF DREAMS

Simon Sien Kang

Illustrated by: Dwight Nacaytuna

To order additional copies of this book, contact:
Xlibris
844-714-8691
www.Xlibris.com
Orders@Xlibris.com

ISBN: Softcover   978-1-6698-1782-6
            EBook   978-1-6698-1781-9

Print information available on the last page

Rev. date: 06/13/2022

Do you ever wonder what happens after we fall asleep? Why do we dream?

What really goes on in our
head when we sleep?

Dreaming is important for us as we need to look deep into our minds and into our imaginative thoughts. Dreaming can help us see our

true desires, wants and needs in life as well as our goals that we need to achieve in life.

Let's start off with the basic stages of sleep. When we sleep, we first enter the NREM also known as non-rapid eye movement sleep STAGE.

4

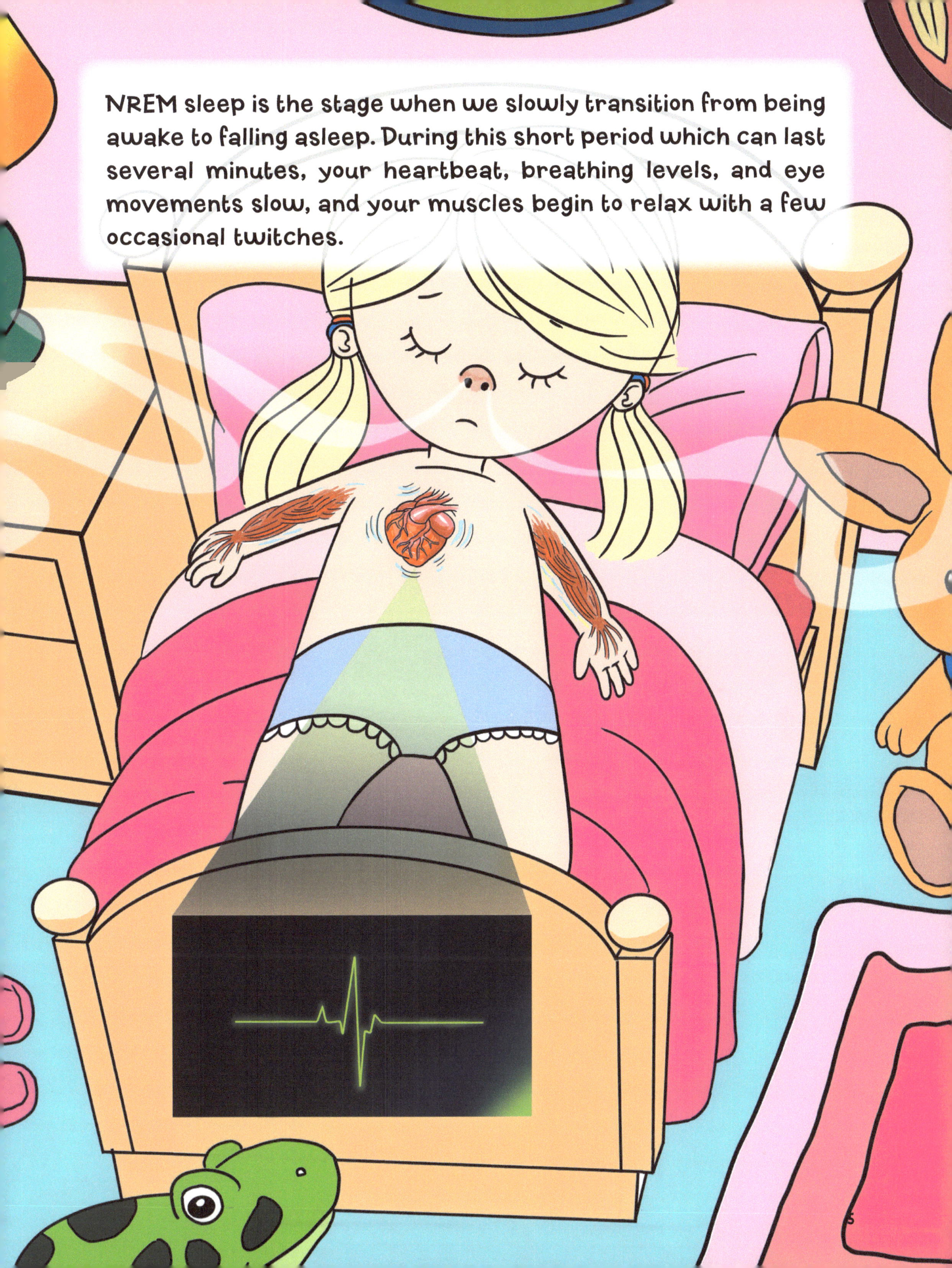

NREM sleep is the stage when we slowly transition from being awake to falling asleep. During this short period which can last several minutes, your heartbeat, breathing levels, and eye movements slow, and your muscles begin to relax with a few occasional twitches.

REM also known as rapid eye movement sleep can occur about 90 minutes after falling asleep. Your eyes move rapidly from side to side behind closed eyelids and your breathing starts to become more
faster and irregular, and your heart rate and blood pressure increase to near waking levels. Most of your dreaming occurs during REM sleep, although some can also occur in NREM sleep. Your arm and leg muscles become temporarily paralyzed, which helps you to keep dreaming.
6

In our mind, dreams can take us somewhere. Places where we've never been before far beyond the limits of our imagination.

We can dream about anything
whether we're young or old.

We can dream
about things that
don't exist like
aliens, monsters
and imaginary
creatures.

We may dream about events that occur in the real world.
PIZZA

Dreams can feel like visions most of the time. They may be a sign of something. Something
that may remind us of the past and warn us of events that may happen in the near future. For example, we may dream of an incident that happens in our daily lives at school or work.

We have lucid dreams, where we have the power to control our dreams in our own minds so we can control our own destiny.

We have
recurring
dreams, where we
may have the same dream
over and over again.

We may have healing
dreams, where we dream
of healing ourselves.

We may have prophetic
dreams where we may see
our future and it may feel
like a vision of the future
for us.

We have daydreams,
which we may dream
about something
wonderful during the day.

At times, we may have nightmares, where we would have to face our deepest fears in life.

We may dream of falling down,
which may symbolize fear.

We may dream of flying, which may lead to success in our lives.

We may dream of water,
which can symbolize
renewal and cleanliness
in our lives.

We may dream of children, which could symbolize that you may have one of your own someday.

We may dream that an angry monster would chase us, which symbolizes trouble in the real world.

We may dream that we are with a loved one like a family member whom we miss.

We may dream of being in a world filled with cartoon characters as we take in what we see from our favorite films and TV shows and we may dream of being together with them.

We may even dream of entering a world from what we read like from a fantasy or adventure book or a comic book.

Dreaming can be a form of escapism and it can allow us to relax our minds. We may dream that we're a superhero or a warrior and it can symbolize that we can become more confident in our lives.

We may have an epic dream, which can change our perspectives on life and appreciate us for who we truly are in life."

For example, we may dream that we are warriors or heroes in life.

Dreams can be stored in our memory forever and it may remain with us for years.

Dreams are good for us as they can allow us to envision a better version of ourselves. Good dreams can also improve our emotions and personalities in life.

You might have nightmares sometimes as well too, but never fear. As long as you remain positive in life, you will always have good dreams.

So remember to dream well the next time you have a good night's sleep and you may feel like a brand new confident person the next day.